Visions Of Life

Charles Anthony Ryan Griffith

authorHOUSE®

AuthorHouse™
1663 Liberty Drive
Bloomington, IN 47403
www.authorhouse.com
Phone: 1-800-839-8640

First published by AuthorHouse 8/11/2011

ISBN: 978-1-4634-0417-8 (e)
ISBN: 978-1-4634-0415-4 (hc)
ISBN: 978-1-4634-0416-1 (sc)

Library of Congress Control Number: 2011908655

Printed in the United States of America

Any people depicted in stock imagery provided by Thinkstock are models, and such images are being used for illustrative purposes only. Certain stock imagery © Thinkstock.

This book is printed on acid-free paper.

Contents

My Vision: Preface To Life

In my youth I looked to my cousin Glen as a role model worthy of emulation. As one of the eldest kids in the neighborhood, Glen was the person that adults trusted to protect the children in the neighborhood, a responsibility he lived up to with great dignity. When Glen entered adulthood and moved away, I assumed his role as the neighborhood keeper. Feeling the magnitude of such immense trust and responsibility resonated with me on a very personal level for I always felt an innate aptitude to lead responsibly. Throughout my life I have served in this role in various capacities: the role of father, brother, son, friend, supervisor. My perspective of leadership rests not in the act of assuming control or dictating orders but rather providing guidance and positive inspiration to those around me. I aim not to change the world but to make a difference in at least one individual's life. It is upon this hope that I offer Visions of Life.

Visions of Life is the product of years of accumulated experience and life lessons learned. Poetry for me is a means to convey my experiences and to share them with others- a gift bestowed upon me by my mother. At the formative age of 19, I boarded a plane to California to reconnect with a person whom I had not really known since childhood- my father. Prior to departure my mother presented me with a book of her poetry. She was a talented poet in her own right, composing descriptive verses of nature and spirituality- most of which she incorporated into recitals for her church. I read verse after verse as the plane soared high above sea level, 3,000 miles toward a new chapter in my life. Though I greatly treasured her gift, at the time I could not fully comprehend its significance. When the plane met the tarmac and I settled into my new home, I tucked her poems away along with the rest of my priceless keepsakes of dated letters and photographs. On birthdays and other special occasions I would reminisce by delving into my hidden relics- spending hours reading through my mother's writings.

As you will soon learn, my gift for writing became apparent at a defining moment in my life. An abrupt awareness of the harsh realities of humankind propelled me into a period of emotional isolation from the outside world.

My only recourse was to put my thoughts onto paper. Powerful visions and revelations inundated my mind and recording them enabled me to make sense of my life and a world plagued with inequities. As my writings amassed I began to realize the impact of my mother's gift of poems- and it is due to her influence that I long to share my incites with others.

The title Visions of Life derives from the manner in which my poems come to me. My process is somewhat trance like, working from the inspiration of a sudden insight and allowing the words to flow from my mind to the paper in a natural flow. I often refer to these glimpses as flashes of life and sometimes serve as interpretations of how I wish for life to be.

On the pages to follow, you, my reader, will be presented with a triad of artistic genres: poems that paint a lyrical portrait of my experiences and revelations, illustrations to provide visualization, and finally, descriptive narratives to lend history to the message conveyed. All of these elements work together to provoke discussion, encouragement, and inspiration. It has become apparent to me that it is not necessarily the atrocity one faces, but the manner in which one accepts what life brings to the table and the faith in ones strength to rise above hardship. It is my sincere hope that Visions of Life will bring to light your inner strength, inspire the will to conquer the obstacles that lie ahead and the desire to celebrate the many gifts life has to offer.

The One

Look deep into the eyes of temptation, but never allow yourself to become another victim...Always tell yourself I'm in control...The dominant one... The one no matter what happens will be successful...I'm the one who will never accept defeat...The strong positive one...The one who makes everyone around me much better...I'm like sunshine-after all I reflect light...Know me for who I truly am and maybe you too can be filled with the ability to conquer all negativity...Always in pursuit of higher learning...Nothing can stop me-for I'm a true believer...Follower of none, but leader of those who choose to seek knowledge.

The One

The One came to me approximately four years ago while staring at myself in the mirror; an action prompted not by arrogance but by the pressure of having to make a decision. While looking into the eyes of the person staring back at me, I realized there is "The One" is each and every person, signifying our ability to reason and to gauge right from wrong, and to make decisions based on our intuitions and definitions of decency. By way of example, it was around this time that a two-year-old girl apprehended a journal of mine and proceeded to scribble in it. As a writer my journals are priceless to me. I could easily have lost my temper with the little girl for vandalizing my journal, but instead, I considered her youth and innocence and deemed her act as a form of personal expression. The moral I garnered was that we all have the power to control our actions and to perceive what may appear to be a negative situation as one that is positive. By looking at myself in this light I was able to see and understand such power, thus fostering the notion that I am the one who can determine the nature of my actions and viewpoints.

Life

I cry tears of icecycles seeing pivotal moments of my life...Trapped in chains of isolation makes me a slave to my evil ways...Begging for repentance from a life long sentence...As I count minutes, hours and days...Placing marks of frustration on walls of resentment...I felt victim to being tempt...Escaping reality by creating fantasies of things that could never be...Wrapped in emotional sath cloth playing harmonious tunes of the blues I'm having... Grabbing onto strings of life...is like going for a roller coaster ride on the edge of a knife-- scarring me permanently, where even blind folks could see my true identity...Looking in the mirror at images created by reflections of denial...Places my soul on trial...Each day I wash my face in hot water of deceit...As I keep building bridges of defeat...Surrounded by illusions of love...Climbing the ladder of success takes me beyond and above...LIFE.

Life

There was a time in my late adolescence when I was still filled with arrogance and deceit, and heading down a rather destructive path. Though this attitude is often concomitant with youth I soon realized that something had to change in my life that I had to reevaluate my actions and disposition. In doing so I found it necessary to break ties with certain friends who were not conducive to such change and who were very well hindering my growth as a responsible individual. This resulted in having to make personal phone calls to end these friendships, a task that was truly difficult but completely worthwhile. Life therefore represents the moment that brought me to such a drastic decision, a moment that forced me to look myself in the mirror, identifying and acknowledging the flaws interfering with the person I wanted to become. I knew from that point onward that I wanted to see only positive qualities when I looked into my eyes, and I wanted to feel hopeful about the path in life I selected. Through relaying my personal transformation it is my hope for my readers to realize that it is acceptable to have flaws, so long as you are willing to change. It is my belief that valor stems from acknowledgement of ones faults and the commitment to correct them; whereas true cowardice resides in those who recognize personal shortcomings yet refuse to take ownership of who they are and who they could become.

Demons

Take a look in my eyes...Journey through my soul-as my life scrolls the struggle unfolds...Righteous the key to happiness or so I was told...I represent now and hereafter-spiritual beliefs keeps me surviving disaster... My family tree consists of permanent black suits (death)...When Grandma died it severe the roots and tainted the fruits...Let the truth be known-at an early age daddy kicked me out of his house-said I was grown...Left searching for an identity...Worldly possessions kept tempting me...Tried my best to do what's right...After a few years I gave up that fight...To be honest I really never saw the light-everyone talks about...Until Satan took my hand and now we both walk the same route...Headed in the wrong direction-still he's the only one that shows me affection...QUESTION: "Does a black man in America stand in an invisible section?" I finally found a way to release the beast in me...Now you know why my decision was so easy...I'm out to please me...Dear God-break these chains of unconsciousness and release me.

Demons

I came from a relatively close-knit family, that was until my grandmother passed away. Her absence in our family left such a tremendous void, forcing my relatives and me to search for answers. It soon became apparent to us that grandma was the glue that kept us together, and without her we were lost. Our lives began to change as a result, beginning with my father's abrupt announcement that I literally had a couple of days to leave his house. I began wondering the streets, striving to figure out my next course of action. Everywhere I turned temptations challenged my will and strength. I needed something or someone to walk with, to guide me through all hardships, but I apprehended that the Devil was the only presence following me. I had a long history of wrong decisions, mistakes that were made possible by the sentiment of feeling invisible to those around me with no one to notice or care about the choices I made. In desperation to save myself, I called upon the assistance of a higher power to grant me the wisdom and strength to pursue a direction in life that would afford success and happiness, devoid of all evil influences. So as it stands, Demons represents my transition from a lost soul to a strong willed individual capable of warding off temptation in pursuit of a righteous path.

Amazing

Can't take this temptation I'm demanding...Standing at the back of the room fanning-away deep thoughts of hot passion...The way that dress fits you-must be the queen of fashion...On love's runway I'm just another plane landing...Mental stimulation I'm expanding...With open arms I'm embracing-visions of us making love is what I'm facing-pacing hardwood floors and engraving...I LOVE YOU-and this feeling is amazing.

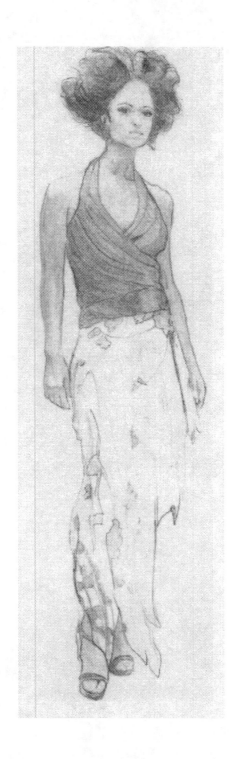

Amazing

I was working at the Oakland Airport teaching training classes to new hires and existing employees. On several occasions I found myself standing before my class of 25 attendants relaying the days while concurrently entertaining random fantasies about my fiancée. I would find myself imaging her in the classroom with the others, wearing an appealing dress and thinking of how amazing she looked and how lucky she made me feel. These fantasies came to mind fairly often but on one particular occasion my mind become so overwhelmed that I actually forgot what I was saying to the class in mid sentence. As a result I was forced to dismiss my students for a five-minute break in hopes of gaining composure and gathering my thoughts. As soon as I had the room to myself I immediately grabbed a piece of paper and wrote a poem to her expressing how amazing she was to me, and how she would always remain in the forefront of my mind no matter the location or circumstance.

Hunted

I dreaded the moment I feared when I stared deep into the eyes of my so called enemy...Hoping to have enough breath to bring him to his death, but really didn't know what to do, cause I was unarmed and he held a twenty two-- caliber stuck in my face...I prayed to the higher power to give me grace...Hoping to see another day...To serve and protect was his way-of total domination that's why we stood segregated into isolation...He gave me a chance to run, but I stood still, cause I didn't wish to be killed...Filled his gun up with bullets-- placed the nozzle in my mouth as he held the trigger and said he would probably pull it...If I didn't do as he asked-I was faced with a tough task...Harass me for two to three hours cause he held the power-firm in his hand as I kept trying to understand...How could this be as I fell on one knee...Thinking of ways to devise a plan-he yelled "Who's the man?" He kept playing with my mind and I knew I was running out of time...For some reason he was distracted-that's when I reacted...Swept him off of his feet, we wrestled for a while until the gun fell out of his hand-now I'm in command...It's time for him to rest in peace, but if I kill him I'll become the beast.

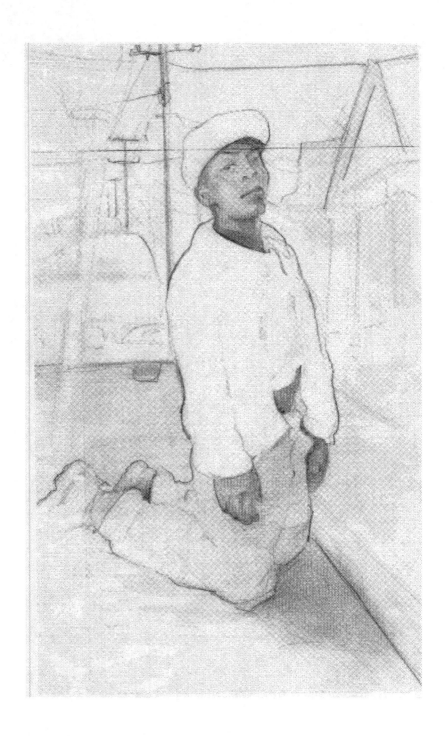

Hunted

Hunted tells the story of one of the most bittersweet, and perhaps the most dramatic moments of my life. I was nineteen years old and just received my driver's license. I entered my father's house to relay the good news, and politely asked for the keys to his car so that I could experience my newfound freedom. He declined though much to my dismay, his best friend, who was visiting at the time, threw me the keys to his luxury car and granted me permission to take it for a test drive. It was truly difficult for me to understand why my own father, who of course knew me very well, would refuse to lend his car to me, but his best friend, who was a mere acquaintance, would throw me the keys to his very expensive car without reservation. Needless to say I did not spend much time pondering this unusual occurrence for the excitement to drive was quite overpowering. I accepted the offer and began driving around the neighborhood. I might have driven as for as a block or two before I noticed a cop car behind me. I was rather apprehensive but decided to keep driving with a cautious eye. I made a right turn, and then a left and the cop was still behind me. At first I thought it nothing more than a coincidence that was until the sirens sounded I pulled over to the curb and the police officer approached the car requesting to see my driver's license. I handed him my permit so that he could process it for verification. Much to my chagrin and bewilderment the officer returned, demanding that I get out of car because he had reason to believe that it was a stolen vehicle. I tried relentlessly to explain the situation but it was of no use, he had me lying face down on the ground. Within minutes five additional police cars surrounded us. Words could never convey how humiliated and degraded I felt, looking up seeing passersby gawking at the dramatic display. I could see and feel them looking at me with contempt and suspicion. A few minutes later I was told to get up from the ground followed by an apology from the police officer for the false accusation. Obviously shaken by the ordeal, I returned to the car, drove two blocks and immediately broke into tears. From that day onward I entered a period of isolation. My days were spent going to and from school and I rarely left the house. This cycle continued for two years, until one day it dawned on me that I couldn't allow one person's stupidity to dictate the course of my life or interfere with my happiness. It is from this hardship that I learned that though injustice will always exist, we cannot allow ourselves to be weakened or broken by the ignorance of others.

Reflections

Look into the eyes of my small kid...See the future one day he's going to be big...Cause I'll guide him in the right direction...Positive is when I look in the mirror and see his reflection...Images of me surpassing the man that I'm trying to be...Constantly praying to God to show him the light...So when he faces his darkest hour he'll shine bright...Over coming any obstacle in life-his instincts are sharp as a knife...Cutting through the roots of his problems-having faith knowing he'll solve em...Standing up for what he believes in and walking away from sin...Taking strides on the path to achieve success-studying hard so he'll pass any test...May God bless his heart and soul...Daddy's love makes him whole.

Reflections

Reflections is the first component of Beautiful, for it was written in honor of my son, Zaryan, born April 1st, 1998. Upon his arrival I tried tirelessly to compose the perfect poem to accurately express my elation and hopes for him, but I could not force the words to meet my expectations. Finally I looked myself in the mirror and thoughts of my father flooded my mind. I asked myself whether or not I surpassed the man my father was and if I was becoming the man that I aspired to be. I realized that I could answer affirmatively to these questions for I've always aspired to do the right thing and to make the best choices. In the aftermath of my revelation I decided that my hope for Zaryan is that he would possess these qualities of mine, and to surpass them with strength, acuity and compassion. Ever since then I have prayed to a higher power for the teachings instilled in Zaryan will reveal reflections of me.

The Wall

Deep in a basement an undertaker does some cremating...
While a lonely boy is masturbating...
Racists are still hating...
Sex addicts keep on inflating - sex toys...
Cross dressing females are really boys - in disguise...
Despite all the tragedies...Silicon breasts are treated like fallacies...
Street walkers are targeted by stalkers...
The black moon symbolized doom...
A police undercover has a secret lover...
Damn - his wife doesn't know its a man!!
So she pretends to blend in with the crowd...
But she'll never hear the truth when the noise is so loud...
The church pastor steals from the collection...
To help find a cure for his infection - of herpes...
He got from Miss C... There's no need to know the rest of the name...
When his wife took the blame...
Mr. White abuses his daughter - with mental slaughter...
Children locked in a cage are filled with rage...
Envious neighbors spy on each other...
While a sister sexually molests her brother...
In the mind of a killer - murder occurs while watching a thriller...
Third degree burns were inflicted...because a grandpa was addicted...
To sniffing propane...Now he feels the pain...
A nice young lady - drives her husband crazy...
By watching talk shows - until he attacks her with blows...
Two to the head - now she's almost dead...
In this neighborhood - there's nothing good...
That's why secrets never fall...
When they're hidden behind the wall.

The Wall

The Wall is essentially based on experience living in an apartment complex in North Oakland. I would often over hear various noises coming from my neighbors on the other side of my wall; sounds relaying pleasure, joy, sorrow, and rage. I would amble through surrounding neighborhoods observing people I passed on my way. Paying close attention to their demeanor, disposition, and gait; wondering who they were, where they were going, what secrets they were hiding, and how they normally act with no one around. Such observations led me to ponder the nature of human behavior. How we as humans tend to build a wall around our selves for the sake of withholding from the world the unflattering, perhaps even menacing facets of our personality. It is in this regard that the implication of The Wall is a metaphor for the multifaceted quality of the human temperament, the invisible wall that shields us from bearing our souls to the world. We often look at other people at face value, but truth be told, we are never fully aware of the depravity or sorrow or struggle that possibly exists within each individual. It is my hope that this poem will spur my reader to ask the question "What is on the other side of that wall?" when passing people on the street or simply sitting in an apartment.

Aside from the content, The Wall is of particular value to me because it is my first poem. It was ten years ago and I had never before considered translating my thoughts in a productive method. Intrigued by the notion of dual personalities, I felt inspired to record my thoughts without hindrance or reservation. Once I tapped into this creative outlet, I gained the confidence to use poetry as a way to communicate the emotions, occurrences, and revelations I would encounter for years to come.

Orgasm

SSSShh...Close your eyes as I take you into the darkness of my candle light seduction...Feel the estacy of my warm hands caressing your cold body with the added affects of the howling wind being highlighted by the occasional flashes of lightning...Oh baby-even before I touched you-I felt you...The ability to stimulate your inner most desire with my presence-motivates me to fulfill your every fantasy...SSSShh-the look on your face from the slow sensual hot oil massages gives me nothing but pleasure-while the sluggish movement of honey trickles down every single curve of your perfect body-that look stimulate the buds on my tongue-but wait-before I taste I must shower you in sizzling bubbles of the finest champagne...Take a sip and allow yourself to be intoxicated with love...The aroma fills the air with joy happiness and excitement all the things I could never enjoy without you...SSSShh...Blindfolded by strips of silk enhances your ability to smell the freshness of tropical fruits-being complimented with a bowl of whip cream...The interaction between your red luscious lips tingle my spine...Oh baby-the firmness of your lovely breast as your nipples stand at attention makes me as hard as I'll ever be...Touch me-feel me-as I seduce you with soft sensuous kisses...SSSShh...Allow me the privilege of drying your wet sultry body with a robe of feathers-as you lay on a tender bed of rose petals...The shivering response from your body as the coldness of ice intertwines with my tongue-give me a taste of the true woman that you are...The loud screams in my ear tells me the time of satisfaction has finally arrived...Now I can enter you...So we both can become one.

Orgasm

I grew up in a household of many male cousins ranging in age from 16-25. As the youngest of the group I would often look to them for guidance and advice. I was at an adolescent stage of sexual curiosity, and my cousins would offer anecdotes on intimacy and what women were looking for in relationships. I always valued their advice and took it to heart, deeming it constructive and somewhat foolproof. Through my subsequent relationships with women, I soon learned that most of what I heard from my cousins was most likely fabricated and/or awfully exaggerated, for women did not seem to behave or react in the manner they so often claimed. In order to gain a better understanding of what women want, I dedicated time to speaking at length with women in my family about their perception of sexuality and companionship. From them I gathered that sexual satisfaction comes not solely from intercourse and sensual acts but from mental stimulation. Thus Orgasm relates to the notion of intimacy that focuses on satisfying your partner mentally before satisfying ones physically urges, primarily through acts or gestures that entice them emotionally. In doing so sexual encounters becomes more than just the climax, resulting in the fulfillment of each partner's body, mind, and soul.

Capital Punishment

The year is 3014...Death Row inmates are being executed with a Guillotine... Cause it's back to basics-One strike and you may have to face it...Thieves that steal from their neighbor may have to do hard labor...Rapist face the wrath when they walk down a long path-without a penis...HIV+ people are being cured on Venus, but there's no coming back-when space crafts are constantly attacked...Convicted felons get cut like melons...Now walking through life scarred is hard...Suicidal personalities who can't cope-get hung by a rope...The homeless are being moved to a new location-after decapitation...Drug dealers who sell that stuff that kills are force to take cyanide pills...Child molesters are the real life jesters-after being injected with a poisonous infective...A sign on the door says "Cancer Cure"-is just another lure...Two shots to the head now that cancer's dead...Mistaken identities are treated like outcast entities...As for car jackers-their bones get break like crackers...Women abusers take a permanent snooze after inhaling chemical ooze-because they strike back...Lethal injection is the remedy for a heart attack...False Prophets get sliced and diced -cause they worshipped the anti-christ...Arsonist get burnt to a crust-then scattered like dust...Ashes to ashes-disobedient children get 25 lashes from a bamboo cane dispite the brutal pain...Racist walked the torture chamber of spiked fists-until they vaporized like mist...Crooked cops get shot-without a bulletproof vest-remaining particles on the wall make a mess...While teenagers that break curfew are boiled like stew...Every day new human sacrifices are made--if you try to evade--this form of capital punishment...That's being approved by the Government.

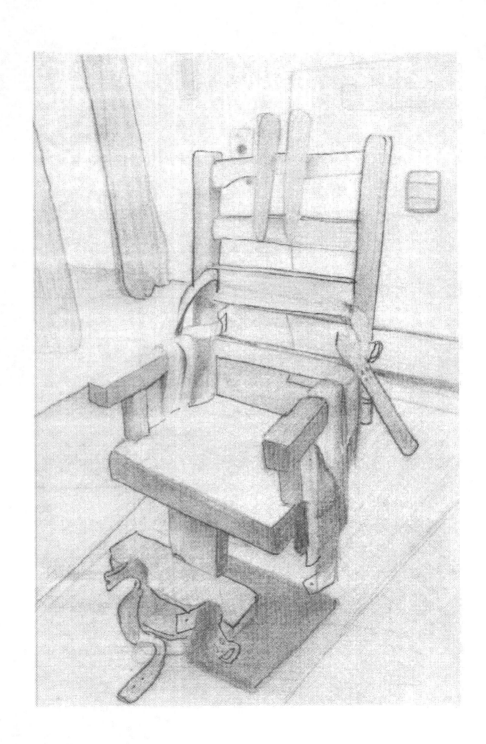

Capital Punishment

The idea for Capital Punishment came to me in the late nineties when a young man was caned in Singapore for on act of vandalism he committed. The event spurred controversy nationwide for many deemed the form of punishment rather drastic for what appeared to be a minor crime. In the aftermath I began to contemplate the nature of capital punishment and the opposing views it often sponsored. It is common knowledge that a distinct line exists between what is right from wrong, and that every criminal or negative act warrants a particular form of penalty. Cognizance of this fact encouraged me to imagine what our world would be like if government officials decided to enforce strict laws restricting our freedom, and punishments for the crimes we commit, such as curfews, hangings, gas chambers, etc. In imaging the world in such a state, I wanted people to think beyond the usual forms of punishment, to compare the sentences that exist today in relation to the severity of what they could be, and to decide which would be better or worse. The second objective I aimed to achieve is encouraging people to think seriously of their actions, for fearing the consequences they might produce.

The Question

Shattered dreams...Where irritation from flies make innocent children scream...Cause there have nothing to eat...So military planes fly over and drop wheat...Is this suppose to be relief? Then here's my question...Why is it so brief? Scampering like animals fighting for food to survive...Hoping they kill each other was how the plan was devise...Demise, in tear drop filled eyes...makes it hard to see the lies...Broken chains...can never replace the pain...FREEDOM is nothing if hardship still remain.

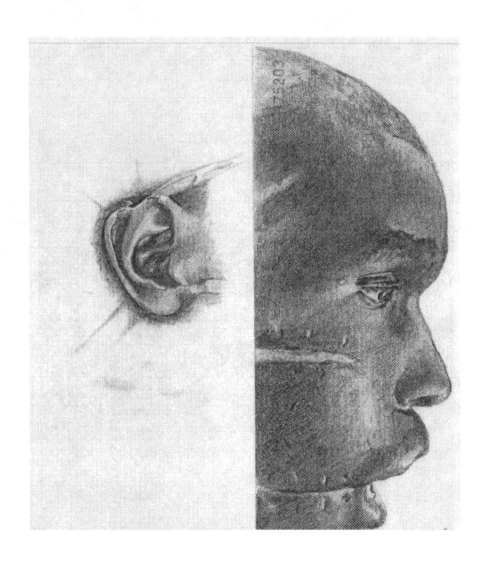

The Question

The Question is my personal commentary on the relationship between the United States and Third World countries. I often become incensed by the thought of our country squandering billions of dollars on futile wars while conflict-ridden countries are struggling to survive in the face of famine and disease. Equally exasperating are the halfhearted humanitarian efforts that this country has made in the past, but with seemingly little intention of following though to ensure that the atrocities abroad are fully extricated and resolved. Failure to follow through with humanitarian relief often exacerbates the situation for it causes further conflict and violence among civilians, such as people fighting for food that is dropped from the sky by US forces. Therefore, The Question serves to express my resentment for those with endless resources refuse to give generously to those who need them most.

Summer Days

What if Parks were made from dark shades of trees that bleed with pain of having no rain...Summer days that sprung green blades of grass...Loud noises from the sound of kids that passed-by - interacting with clear blue water from the reflection of the sky...Barbecue grills that spill - sweet smells of meat that can fill - tables of family laughter - after fun and games - Clouds of aroma form from burning desire of open flames... Char broiled memories of...Birds chirping, Cheerleaders rehearsing...Old church ladies going "Please no cursing"...Ice cream vendors dispersing...I SCREAM..."Hamburgers and hot dogs while playing ball is part of the American DREAM"...WAKE UP!! Tired from taking a cross country trip...Relaxing in a tent snacking on chips and dip...Flavors of a rainbow can never be seen...Except through the eyes of every human being...Short skirts smiles and flirts - with hawaiian shirts - in cargo jeans - ankle socks and fly kicks...Grease lips search for napkins and toothpicks...While lemonade quenches thirst...After being exhausted we sit on benches first... Watching wind blow kites out of sight...Sky divers jump without fright... Clowns and Mimes amazes us with delight...Smiling faces shine bright... Glowing - Frisbee throwing...Dogs chasing...Joggers pacing...Bikers racing...Lovers facing - Kissing each other - Family reunion I can't wait to see my brother...Drunk uncle acting silly trying to catch my sister...Auntie yelling "Is everyone ready for water twister"...Grab your super soakers... Let's attack those chain smokers...Get rid of all the jokers - in the brand new deck of cards...Dominoes being slammed hard...Sshhh...Look...Sign says quiet please - Reserve for anyone trying to read a book and be at ease... What if Parks were made from Sunsets...Honeymooners skinny dipping getting wet...Toasting before sipping moet... Bubbles of surprise...Parties until sunrise...Have you wondering why...We continue to crave...HOT SUMMER DAYS.

Summer Days

I was sitting in a park on a beautiful afternoon, taking notice of all the surrounding activities; teenagers playing basketball at a near by court, families convening for a peaceful picnic, my son playing with seemingly endless energy that only children possess. I decided to document my observations so I settled underneath a tree and began to write. A lady stood close by in near amazement, either by the sight of my conviction to write or by the manner in which I repeated the words faintly aloud to myself. Unable to complete the piece I set it aside for another day. A few months later I was in Spokane, Washington on business. The temperature in the region was dreadfully cold and I couldn't help but long to be basking in that beautiful summer day again. Living amid the snow and freezing climate I began to appreciate how we spend the days of summer, and how much we often take them for granted until the winter months draw near. Therefore, Summer Days is my attempt to capture and preserve the carefree and tranquil spirit of the season.

12 Steps To Success

Let's take a trip down memory lane and remain sane...Deep thoughts are growing.

(1) Your eyes are open, but you focus on not knowing...Concentrating on what if...Now you're on the wrong path...Probably took a left.

(2) Headed in the wrong direction...Can't make a positive U-TURN on a one way street with no intersection.

(3) Negative reflections have you living a lie...Claiming to be sober isn't going to do you good if you're high.

(4) Wondering why....Your life is on a down hill? Praying to God and living for Satan will definitely get you kill.

(5) Will you live to see another day? Having the wrong friends can lead you astray.

(6) Must I continue to show you what's right...Cowardly hearts give up without staying to fight.

(7) Is this the way that you choose? Saying you can't is like saying you'll rather loose.

(8) Bruise egos never know and are always quick to let go... Hold on to what you believe in and refrain from sin.

(9) There's a thin line between love and hate...Anticipate setbacks and you'll elevate.

(10) Stimulate the mental by reading and eliminate internal bleeding (pain).

(11) Seek knowledge of things you didn't know and allow yourself to grow.

(12) Accept defeat...Learning from mistakes will help you retreat...

So when you finally taste SUCCESS it will always be sweet.

12 Steps to Success

As the title infers, 12 Steps...to Success is reminiscent of the Alcoholics Anonymous support program fashioned to assist members in conquering addictions. In considering the nature of this type of therapy, I decided to create my own blueprint for success formed from an evaluation of my life. In doing so it was incumbent of me to identify the most important qualities that I deemed important for success most of which were often achieved by relinquishing the negative influences in my life. Much to my dismay, 12 Steps...To Success afforded one of the most rewarding gifts. I had the poem lying out and a woman happened to read it. She was immensely touched by the poem, so much so that she expressed interest in obtaining a copy for her son, believing that it could possibly inspire him to turn his life around. The gesture was deeply moving for it represented the only goal I hope to achieve, that which is touching just one person through my writing.

Change

I need change...
But I'm not talking about a quarter, two nickels and a dime...
I'm talking about what people perceive in their minds...
I need change...
Like four seasons in a year...
Change like having a white man walk through a black neighborhood without fear...
I need change...
That takes away assumptions of hate...
Change that allows us to have or intellectual conversation or debate...
Change that makes us elevate...
I need change...
Like walking in a store and not having people think I'm going to say, "Put your hands up"
The type of change that if you fall...I'll help you stand up...
I need change...
Like not believing if I get her pregnant I'm gonna leave..
Why would I? Without my kid I can't breathe...
I need change...
Like going from Bush to Clinton back to Bush...
Change like if I need motivation you'll give me a push...
I need change...
Like colors in a rainbow...
The kind of change that gives us enough knowledge to glow...
I need change...
Like coming home from work taking a shower and putting on clean clothes...
Change like an epidemic free world where no one's exposed...
I need change...
Like watching a green light turn amber then red...
Change that makes you understand what's going on in my head...
I need change...
Like adolescent teenagers going through puberty...
Change that acknowledges the only solution is unity...
I need change...
Like switching channels on a TV...

The type of change that creates enough trust for you to believe me...
I need change...
Like turning pages in a book...
Change that attracts you to someone's mind not the look...
I need change...
Like I'm approaching you don't have to hold on to your purse...
Because of the way I'm dress you don't speculate the worst...
I need change...
Like going from night to day...
Change like knowing life isn't a game, so we shouldn't have to play...
I need change...
Like the difference between nine and six...
Change that eliminates illegal drugs from society, so no one needs a fix...
I need change...

51

Change

One afternoon I was searching through my pocket for change to feed a parking meter. I became increasingly frustrated when I realized I came up short, and in the process I kept thinking to myself "I need change, I need change, I NEED CHANGE!". Then suddenly I reasoned beyond my frustration and outside of my literal interpretation of "change" as a few coins but to a more figurative association. I began wondering what I needed to change about my life or personality or attitude, and soon came to the conclusion that every person needs "change" in his or her life. Therefore, Change came about from this revelation and for the purpose of encouraging people to question what they need to alter in their attitudes or everyday lives to achieve a more contented existence.

Remember

Like wind blowing through the trees on spring days-kids play hop scotch and jump rope...Hide and seek at night isn't a joke if you're filled with fright...Street lights beam off the domino table...We all crowd around Mrs. Jones house cause she's the only one with cable-TV...Boys in the back yard building a Tee Pee...Girls playing make believe- after running for the ice cream truck it was hard to breathe...Mom yelling out names-no telling who took the blame-when we reached home-she usually left us all alone-to go visit her friend down the street- while we eat sardines and crackers with lemonade-better wash those dishes with cascade...Before she came back we hid the strap-couldn't deal with that pain on our backs...Strangers knocking at the front door-while we hid under the bed just to make sure... Older boys outside bragging about girls-spraying activator on hair to keep the curls...If you don't have a pair of bell bottom pants-you probably shouldn't go to the dance...Remember those days.

Remember

I consider 1982 to be one of the best years of my life. I was eleven years old, still filled with innocence and curiosity. Life was uncomplicated and carefree for my days were spent not in front of the television but playing outside with the neighborhood friends watching men play dominos under street lights and us playing childhood games for hours on end. It was a time where we were not corrupt by outside influences so much so that our parents could leave for the afternoon and we would feel the excitement of having the house to ourselves yet still fearful of a stranger knocking on the door. I deem '82 an entertaining year, nothing outrageous to speak of but the sheer simplicity of being young and untroubled. Remember is not only my way of capturing my affection of this time but to encourage my readers to recollect on experiences and years in their lives that are positive and heartwarming. I believe that remembering such feelings will enable to us to achieve them once more and to find solace in the memories we hold dear.

Visions

Sailing on slave slaughtered waters where my forefathers were tortured-makes it hard to enjoy this luxury cruise...Visions of them being abused by the hands of angry white men...Standing in front of terrified children...Flipping whip lashes off backs-constant attacks in mud huts...Calling black queens sluts-trapped in chains with no escape-often led to rape...Mix breeds of unwanted seeds-as wombs bleed with pain of no redemption...Not to mention-tears of revenge filled the eyes of faithful close mouth wives-made it hard to reveal the truth-as racist youth-watched the hatred their parents created in the form of brutality-was everyday reality...As innocent people partied their lives away-it's hard to say-stuck with sea sickness of the fact-pain was inflicted simply because they were black...Hard work would never pay on extremely hot days...Toiling in the sun was never fun-as sweat poured into open flesh wounds...I see visions of them tribal dancing to the same tunes...Crying tears of rejoice-chanting words of inspiration with the same voice...Humming-sweet melodies as drums beat-raised clinched fist could never be a sign of defeat...Stressed out-I hear screams and shouts-sounds of rattling chains in the night-survival fights-to the death-cause Massa and his men were trying to take the last breath...Incest was his way of maintaining white supremacy-at his daughters discrepancy...As north winds blow spirals of fear through my hair-grease bodies on showcase-after they were captured from being chased...Erased all doubt-of getting back out...I see visions-of incisions-done with sharp knives-castrated scarred lives-of men who once were kings-had everything to loose-after being abused...Chose not to rebel-scared of getting their tongues cut out if they didn't tell-whether or not they were part of the plot-to over throw-was called maintaining even flow-of slaves who were considered brave-got lynched and hung from a tree...I see-visions-of men on horses hiding behind sheets-burning crosses in the streets...Destroying cultivated land-made it hard to understand...Why they would want us to trade the roots to our soul-by wagering us for gold-found underground railroads-opened new doors of opportunity-so they could stay forever free...I continue to see Visions.

Visions

I watched the films Amistad and Titanic consecutively. Though these two movies are obviously disparate in subject matter, it became apparent to me they shared a common theme that focused on imminent tragedy. In watching Titanic I imagined myself among the other desperate passengers and how I would react. Flashbacks of Amistad suddenly coalesced with my visions of the Titanic tragedy and realized that passengers on either ship were essential experiencing similar fear and torture. The realization of such torture became somewhat tangible a few weeks later while walking along the Berkeley Marina. I looked out across the water and was suddenly able to visualize ships sailing along the horizon. It was then that my mind seemed to drift from my body into a trance-like state, from which I began to envisage the horror and torment experienced on the slave ships. As an African American I come from a lineage of ancestors who did live such a horrid experience, and it felt as though an ancestor whom I never met was talking to me so that I could image his or her suffering. Such an experience is exemplary of the trance like state that constitutes my writing process. I am the medium of my poems in all actually. Rarely do I ever force my method of composition for something almost always seems to take over my mind and my body, allowing the words to flow freely on to the page. Therefore the sole motivation behind Visions is credited to the moment at which a seemingly otherworldly presence temporarily took hold of my consciousness so as to recount their hardship through me.

The Epidemic

First let's create a cure, but one thing remains sure...Scientific seal of approval...Never give it out-destroy all evidence-sworn through secrecy by word of mouth...Now here's what all the madness is really all about... Started out in third world countries-unidentified laboratories-began by injecting Islanders like junkies...Cause the Government wasn't satisfied with testing monkeys...They never used procrastination when they decided to blame it on Haitians...Must be the leaders of an Aryan Nation... Annihilation of anyone that wasn't Caucasian-added to the equation... Simultaneously this genocidal decision was indorse by the wealthy...So called unhealthy relationships were targeted next for anyone who was involved with the same sex...Questions concerning genetics-developed around homosexuality dividing the people judgements into individuality... Reality was blurred when all the prejudice occurred...Gay men and women were treated like outcast, but that hostility didn't last-when it affected the heterosexual community-out cries of bring back unity-the only know antidote...Still the people didn't wish to cope...Dope addicts deaths were pre-arrange through free contaminated needle exchange...Isn't it strange-how politicians would do anything to try and conceal the truth, even by infecting innocent youth...The proof really isn't hard to find when the real sickness can be found in the President's mind.

The Epidemic

The Epidemic is a personal commentary on the AIDS crisis in America and the controversy surrounding it. I became amazed at how each party tirelessly strove to find blame for the disease when in reality discovering a cure should have been the primary concern among the worried populace. In attempt to bring awareness of the disease I conducted research the library at Laney College, gleaning facts pertaining to the origin of AIDS, the effects it has on it's victims, and how it is contracted from one person to another. My findings led to a personal belief that the government is in fact cognizant of the purported "AIDS mystery" and thus withholding such knowledge by placing blame on homosexuality. In essence, my goal for The Epidemic was to not only recount the controversy and to provide factual statistics, but also to bring general consciousness to people concerning the power held by our government to employ deceitful mechanisms that merely perpetuate prejudices and obscure truth.

If

If by chance we could sundance underneath the moonlight...Shinning bright-wouldn't need no candles-to blow out love handles sea breeze-caressing our bodies places our minds at ease...Tease me with stimulation of the mental might be more essential to the imagination...Close your eyes and see the different variations of love kaleidoscopes...Hope to fill your presence with spiritual essence-flavors of a queen-similar to the smell of a cocoa bean...Grinding to sexophone instrumentals-with energy like vitamins and minerals...If-I could place you on a pedestal-surrounded by petals-from roses exposes my inner most-feelings to be the perfect host...Complimentary champagne-forever leaves my heart stain...Don't it all seem ironic...If-we continue to sip some love tonic.

If

A friend and I were at the beach one evening after spending the afternoon touring the sites of San Francisco. We stood in the sand on what appeared to be the edge of the world and I couldn't help but feel somewhat overwhelmed by the romantic ambiance. If was my attempt to capture this mood, the feeling of walking along the ocean with the moon serving as the sole light source and crashing waves providing the ambient soundtrack. It occurred to me that witnessing such an experience is quite similar to that of an orgasm, but more so of an emotional one that heightens your senses and is only fully appreciated when shared with someone for whom you truly desire. Though aside from the atmospheric elements that often contribute to amorous feelings, it is essentially the feeling of love and experiencing it with someone you love that is worth capturing and attaining.

Reality

My Grandma had her leg amputated...
Two days after I celebrated my 30th belated...
Grandpa's still fill with hatred...
Cause half his stuff is out dated...
Life's being played out like R-rated...
Graphic as stated...
It's hard to see the truth when your eyes are faded...
I placed flowers on the grave of my brother David...
In this concrete jungle I don't know what being safe is...
Inscribed on his tombstone "I hope you find where the quite place is"...
I watched an innocent girl being violated...
Heartless guys laugh after being stimulated...
Across the street a topless bar is being vacated...
Strippers hiding from cops yelling, "we made it"...
Death's around the corner it's hard to evade it...
Minus 40 degrees and a homeless man is naked...
Robbery at the liquor store cashier screaming "take it"...
A guy thinks his girl is having an orgasm, but she fakes it...
Another brother dies and there're having a shoot out close to where the wake is...
Each day I ask myself am I going to make it?
Cause reality keeps getting much more complicated...

Reality

I was ambling aimlessly along a local street, observing the individuals and activities take place as I passed. In my solitude I walked by men harassing women, hookers soliciting customers, and countless acts reflecting the current state of the world. As I continued to walk in solitude, I envisioned individual voices speaking to me at different times at different locations, and speculated on what these tortured souls would say or reveal about their life. The coupling of the scenes that I witnessed and the respective, though imagined, confessions, signify an outcry of what is occurring in reality. As desperately as we might try to believe, the truth remains that a utopian society will never exist. Our idealized visions of life will always be categorically dismissed by the atrocities and hardships occurring around us. In other words, Reality is the awareness of reality.

Beautiful

It's hard to relinquish this feeling of existence-that lies within the eyes of my daughter's essence...Crown jewels glow from her presence...Sparking spiritual royalty...Undivided attention-inspired by loyalty...Reflections of a Queen is her true identity...Destiny of her birth was meant to be...Princess of earth...She rules with reality.

Beautiful

Beautiful is dedicated to and inspired by my daughter, Zakara. Moments before her arrival on September 25, 2002, I was sitting in the delivery room ruminating on what I could write to accurately express how I felt at that moment and how elated I was for her to enter my life. For months I often envisioned what she would look like and I knew that she would be breathtaking- but Zakara came into the world even more beautiful than I imagined. I had a feeling that the moment was soon approaching where the words would suddenly spill out on to the page, uncontrollably. So much so that I nearly forced myself to compose the perfect poem: the ideal tribute to Zakara yet for some unknown reason the words refused to flow from my consciousness. It was not until a few months after her birth that the inspiration finally surfaced. The result was not the extensive epic I had anticipated, but rather a simple, crisp interpretation of my adoration for her. Beautiful, in its simple and effortless phrases, serves as the perfect summation of Zakara and is better than anything I had previously anticipated.

The Never Ending Story

For reasons beyond my control I'm out on parole...Held captive for committing a crime I didn't do...I'll remain true-to myself...See I'm the only one who I believe deserves an explanation...So when they said...

"Guilty" I accepted incarceration...I figure it was time to find another way being confined all day...Took the lesson of life's blessing, but never thought for once of confessing...See I wanted them to believe-that the system allows us to breathe...From one day I was standing in the Police spot light...Even before I was considered a suspect they pulled the noose around my neck skin tight-didn't fight...Instead I surrendered and didn't give those pigs a chance to be offended...For killing me they'll probably get their badges suspended- for two to three days, cause that crime never pays...Pacing my cell where my father walked is hard to tell-if my kids can escape this-form of brutality I'm faced with...Even though my back is against the wall, I'll never fall...I stand strong in my beliefs-so why show grief...Signs of a rejected man who doesn't understand...They keep trying to frustrate me, but I'll remain calm-plus the gun used for evidence was never found in my palm...Yet I was held without bail-to prolong my stay in a filthy jail...Tell me what kind of justice is this-where innocent victims are accused of drug business...I guess it's because of the clothes I wear that makes uneducated mind stare.

The Never Ending Story

There is a courtyard at Laney College where students convene between classes. On many occasions I was of witness to fellow students passing judgment on those walking through the square; surveying the appearance, gait, and demeanor to form inferences on the person without having known them I soon fell victim to the same kind of scrutiny while shopping at a local store. As I wandered the aisles I noticed a store manager close behind and keeping close watch of my every move. As I reached for my wallet he approached me and spotted the amount of cash I had on me. The manager's attitude changed the moment he realized that I had money, whereas before he assumed from my appearance that I was in the store for ulterior motives. Therefore, it is from this observable fact and personal experience that The Never Ending Story stems, for no matter how hard we try to negate stereotypes, certain people will continue to judge others based on appearance alone.

The Lesbian

If looks could kill Ill be dead...You storing at me I see the vengeance in your head...The way your eyes roll-I can read your thoughts as if they were written on a scroll...The funny thing about all this-we have no memories to reminisce...How could you hate a complete stranger, I probably would never understand-or is it that you hate every man...I have no problem with you dating the same sex...All I'm asking for is that we show each other respect...What have I done to offend you-I apologize...Is it the way I tagged your lover with my eyes? I really can't help the fact that I'm attracted to all women-even if they don't date men...So please excuse my actions once again-but I really didn't mean to cause you any pain.

The Lesbian

While riding on BART from Richmond to the Oakland Airport I noticed a handful of women board the train. I caught the eye of one attractive woman in the crowd. We engaged one another in a silent, yet innocent flirtation- she looking at me with a coquettish smile and I looking at her with interested eyes. I soon noticed the woman sitting next to her glowering at me with disapproval. Naturally this left me confused seeing that nothing substantial had occurred. The women soon disembarked at the McArthur station, and at that moment it dawned on me that is was the weekend of Gay Pride in San Francisco. Realizing this made me infer that the two women were actually partners and the resentful glare was provoked by my playful glances toward the woman's girlfriend. The Lesbian is thus inspired by this event. Though quite humorous, it is essentially an apology to the lady for unwittingly flirting with her lover, with the action justified by my attraction to all women. Furthermore, The Lesbian also serves a statement of wanting individuals to have respect for one another in every regard.

Angel

Dear God: Could I have a moment or two-to yell at you-scream at you... Please forgive me for being an angry man, but there're certain things I could never understand...Why is it that way? Seems like only innocent people pay...Oh father today I come before you in pray...Of all the things I could ask for-it would really be nice-if you would give me another chance at life...So I could offer it to a friend from the bottom of my heart...Cause I'd rather see her happy and have my world fall apart.

Remembering her smile is like having light in the dark-and even though we both been through a lot...Embracing each other would make the pain stop...Let's forever wipe away the teardrops.

Angel

I was in the midst of a very difficult time in my life following a painful breakup. My days were spent at work, forcing myself to be uplifting for it was my responsibly provide guidance and support to the other employees. I found it exceedingly trying to put forth an air of happiness while deep within I felt nothing but grief and heartache. I believed that my charade was fairly convincing, that was until a lady, by the name of Lily, confronted me. She sensed my unhappiness and once approached, I adamantly denied her harmless accusation. From that point onward I avoided her, slipping into a state of denial and refusing to confront my depression. A few months had passed before I gained courage to speak with her face to face. I confessed to my concealed sadness, and turn she divulged her grief over the recent loss of her grandmother. Lily and I became instant friends. She made such a vast impression on me especially with her heartfelt discussions about life.

Lily eventually left the company to work elsewhere and we subsequently lost contact. One day, some time following Lily's departure. I ran into her sister who informed me that Lily was diagnosed with cancer. I immediately fell to my knees when I heard the news, completely overcome with shock and sadness. Lily was always so healthy and full of life, it just did not seem possible for her to have such a debilitating illness. I spent the next few days digesting the awful news and questioning why bad things always happen to good people. In effort to find solace I prayed to a higher power to bestow upon me another chance at life so that I could enrich the life of my ailing friend. The result was Angel, which I wrote for the purpose of expressing how she would always be an angel to me. I delivered the poem to her in person with the intention of giving encouragement, though quite typical of Lily; it was she who ended up lifting my spirits through consistent laughter and levity. Angel is hence dedicated to Lily, for her courage, her grace, and her everlasting radiance.

To Kill A Black Man

I wanna kill a black man...
For not knowing he's the original man...King of his own land...
I wanna kill a black man...
For abusing his Queen...Getting frustrated, cause he can't achieve his dream...
I wanna kill a black man...
For deserting his kids...Now they face reality not knowing who daddy is...
I wanna kill a black man...
For not understanding the truth...When all he has to do is look in the mirror to find proof...
I wanna kill a black man...
For acting like he knows it all...Trying to front when his back is against the wall...
I wanna kill a black man...
For standing on the corner all day selling dope...Giving up on life cause he can't cope...
I wanna kill a black man...
Far walking away and turning his back on hope...
I wanna kill a black man...
For not believing in the system...Yelling out profanity thinking he's a victim...
I wanna kill a black man...
For dropping out of College...Trying to educate me when he lacks knowledge...
I wanna kill a black man...
For not having a job...Can't support himself so he goes out and rob...
I wanna kill a black man...
For not searching for his roots...Has no money in his pockets, yet he's in the latest designer suits...With timberland boots...Some body better tell him...Fool you ain't cute...
I wanna kill a black man...
For trying to be a con artist...Looking all mean thinking he's the hardest...
I wanna kill a black man...

For disrespecting the next man...Doesn't believe in love cause he's after sex...Damn...

I wanna kill a black man...

For not knowing his rights...Police approach him and he's willing to fight...

Now he's hand cuffed on his way to jail...

I wanna kill a black man...

For not being able to prevail...

I wanna kill a black man...

For always expecting a hand out...Thinking material things makes him stand out...

I wanna kill a black man...

For being lost...Because of self destruction now he pays the cost...

Can't manage his own life, yet he wants to be boss..

I wanna kill a black man...

For not knowing where I'm coming from...Only if he could see through my eyes he'd stop acting dumb...

I wanna kill a black man...

For having to run...Knowing he's innocent, yet he retaliates with a gun...

I wanna kill a black man...

For not aiming for the sky...Can't remember anything cause he's drunk or high...

I wanna kill a black man...

For wondering why...He has to base his life on a lie...

I wanna kill a black man...

For stealing my car and going for a joy ride...But if I kill a black man...It's like committing suicide.

To Kill a Black Man

The news today is fraught with accounts of bombings, murders, national and international suffering, etc. Everywhere you look someone is staring fate in the face, usually at the hands of another individual. In observing the ubiquity of violence in the world, I could not help but wander when it would all end and what would be the catalyst to lead to much needed change. In doing so I attempted to categorize crime and thought about what, if anything, would force me to take the life of another human being. The result culminated in To Kill a Black Man, which focuses not on the demise of an actual person, but stereotypes that have so often been associated with violence and crime. To Kill a Black Man ultimately fostered a personal revelation, if I was to take a life, it would have to be mine for I would never be responsible for anyone's death but my own.

The End

I cry tears of blood...Seeing floods...
Land washed away....
Having lightning flashbacks of better days...
As thunder rolls...
Scriptures of kings were once written on scrolls...
Covered underneath dessert storms...
Dead Sea water remains warm...
I'm getting cold shivers from raindrops...
As I'm walking through an intersection where all life stops...
Vision of cemeteries...As a disciple my mission varies...
Seeing people die for religion is the only thing that's scary...
If I could kill the past...The truth would be the only thing I'd never bury...
Digging deep inspiration with words that are destined to be legendary...
Causing earthquakes when I shake symptoms of being greedy...
I'm sharing food for thought; here's a free plate for the needy...
Mind stays complicated but hard to read like graffiti...
Inscribed on walls like reflections of Nefertiti...
Bones lay motionless in a gold tomb...
Seen through the eyes of a child that was never concealed in a womb...
Who died and was resurrected on the third day...
Prophecies of December 25th being his birthday...
There's no celebration of life when death comes in the worst way...
Plagues fill the land and make the curse stay...

The End

It is universally understood that everything must come to an end. My interpretation of such a nation is exemplified in the aptly titled poem, The End. The ending of a chapter in ones life and the beginning of a new could evoke both positive and negative feelings and can be subject to various interpretations. In my experience the end is to be seen as the conclusion of a negative situation and the beginning of a constructive one; the end of abuse initiates the beginning of freedom, the end of addiction fosters the beginning of sobriety, the end of heartache gives way the beginning of happiness, the end of life leads to the beginning another. Such transformations are evident in The End through recounting my hypothetical walk through revelations where everything negative is coming to an end and the promise of a new beginning is on the threshold of fruition. The revelations are set amid storms floods, and gore, yet as I walk through such destruction I'm struck with the relieving sensation that redemption is just on the horizon. Though my portrayal of the end is biblical in nature, it permeates far deeper than any linear connotation. The message is applicable to anyone suffering from distressing circumstances, that which is those who endure life's hardships may look forward to the joy they so rightfully deserve.